BATTERY ACID BRAIN

BATTERY ACID BRAIN

by A.M. Wegelin

Paperclip Publishing, LLC
Chandler, AZ

Battery Acid Brain

Published by: Paperclip Publishing LLC

Editor: Abigail T. Matteson
Cover Design: Keenan S. Peebles
Interior Typography: Hannah Thigpen

Library of Congress Control Number: 2022939674

ISBN: 979-8-88589-193-6 (paperback)

ISBN: 979-8-88589-209-4 (hardcover)

ISBN: 979-8-88589-194-3 (eBook)

Printed in Rephen Printing, Co. LTD in Guangzhou and the United States of America

First Printing: 2022

Paperclip Publishing LLC
3800 W Ray Road Suite 5
Chandler, AZ 85226

www.paperclippublishing.com

To Jarrett, you always believe in me.

CONTENTS

Prologue

"We will release her today only on one condition."

"Anything, I just want to take her home."

"She needs to see a psychologist. She refused medication here, but she needs some form of continuous treatment."

"...A psychologist? How often?"

"At least once a week. If not more. Also, you need to stop leaving your daughter home alone."

"Are you kidding me?! This place drained our savings! Not to mention the hospital bills to pump her stomach...How am I supposed to afford this?"

"Holly is suffering from extreme manic and depressive episodes that suggest Bipolar 1 Disorder. She has anxiety-based hallucinations and disorganized thoughts. This is not her first suicide attempt, and if you don't get her help and a proper diagnosis...this won't be her last. I suggest you find a way before something worse happens than a 51/50...I mean, you can always commit her and we can do more here—"

"That won't be necessary. I'm taking my daughter home. She's only seventeen for God's sake."

I hear footsteps coming toward me and I peel my ear away from the door, springing back into the plastic chair I am supposed to be sitting in. I look down in shame as the door swings open and my dad bursts through.

"Let's GO, Holly." He grabs my wrist off my lap and pulls me toward the two doors that I know lead to my freedom. The doors that I truly know will lead me back to my destruction.

1

No one gives a fuck about your favorite color. People may ask with a feigned look of interest, but in all actuality, they are just waiting to open their rubbery mouths to spew out from their moist tongues their favorite color, because what everyone really wants is just to tell you THEIR favorite color. No one honestly cares about your favorite color and they certainly don't care why it's your favorite color. So don't even bother sharing that part because they aren't actually listening. They are just thinking how damn special their favorite color is and how special they are for liking it even though at least five-hundred million other people think exactly the same thing. Everyone is so desperate to share their story. To share their ever-so interesting bits and pieces because they truly believe they are incredibly special and they desperately want you to believe they are too. No one is special. And no one gives a fuck about your favorite color.

I am tripping extremely hard right now. I definitely should not have taken an entire eighth of mushrooms. This is too much psilocybin for me to currently handle in the state of mind I'm in. I have been sitting on this toilet for too long, watching the peeling walls stretch upwards and the tiles vibrate beneath my feet, as if they want to jump right out of the grout. It feels as if anything behind me does not exist, if I were to reach my hand around I would touch nothing but an empty void. My already alien-like eyes must be wide as saucers as I stare around me, deep in this horrifying train of thought that everyone is a selfish cunt. Even me…I'm probably the most selfish one I know, actually. Constantly asking people questions just so I can share my opinions and answers. I want to be the special one. *You're not special Holly,* this thought echo in my brain. Banging against the walls of my skull, causing me to grit my teeth at this imagined pain. I press my palm against the granular wood of the door in front of me in this cheap studio apartment, feeling the plasticity of the white paint on my skin. The door is throbbing, as if it were trying to break free from this reality of my mind. I hate it. It hates me back. I need out of this pure white prison bathroom before I claw my skin off. I dig my fake nails into the soft flesh of my cheeks, the real nail underneath so yellow, brittle, and broken from all the stress and medication that I covered them with plastic in some hopes of normalcy. Their bright red color reminds me of blood right now and as I pull them from my face, I panic that I broke skin. Screaming, I slam my forehead into the door.

"...Holly?"

The door knob starts to turn. Terrified that the door has become sentient and is readying itself to kill me for attacking it, I sink to my knees and begin to openly weep.

"PLEASE DON'T HURT ME."

The knob stops turning abruptly. "What the fuck are you talking about? You've been in the bathroom for, like, twenty minutes. I gotta piss... Are you okay?"

How could a door possibly have to piss? My brain starts going a million miles a minute. *What's happening?* I rub my eyes hard until fractals pop into my eyelids. "Holly, open the fucking door or I'm coming in."

I know that voice. "....Sam?"

"Of course it's Sam. Who else would it be? We are in my apartment."

In a moment of intense relief to be free of this bathroom hell and with something familiar, I swing the door open and jump into Sam's arms. I have never been more happy to see his goofy, crooked smile and feel his creepy, boney arms wrapped around me.

"SAM, your bathroom, it's no good."

"It's a fucking bathroom, Holly."

"Sam, SAM. No one CARES about your favorite color."

"Oh, jeez...you might be right but you should really be worrying about all the snakes in the room right now." I stare blankly at him in horror as he snorts laughing and shuts the bathroom door behind him. Alone now in this claustrophobia inducing room, the television flickers, making the ever-changing colors on the walls more sinister. I back up slowly, looking around with caution as the now demonic colors on the wall slither into each other. My heel hits the bed and I fall back, my eyes now fixed on the stucco ceiling.

The noise I hadn't registered from the TV before is now blaringly loud, but no voices or particular sounds are discernible. The stucco on the ceiling creates small shadows with every flash of the TV, and with every flash they start to stretch and stretch and stretch and—

"Jesus, Holly, how much did you take, 5 grams?" I snap up as Sam stands in front of the bed with the faint sound of a toilet flushing in the background. My eyes focus on his as I contort my face into what must be something friendly. The shadows crawl above me.

"I've taken enough, now let's go outside and have a cigarette."

"Ohhhh, we can't. Outside doesn't exist anymore." Sam, in his own state of intoxication, doesn't realize the turmoil I'm in and darkly grins at me.

"No, no Sam. We NEED to go outside. I NEED a cigarette."

"Outside is gone. They got rid of it. The only thing that exists is this apartment. Outside is under construction." He steps even closer and his grin becomes unbearably large, almost as if the lower half of his face was entirely teeth. My heart beats into my throat. The feeling of dread of what waits for me on the ceiling is growing. The television's flashing and writhing becomes a sinuous monster with one intention of devouring me whole and Sam's face only becomes more like a wolf in sheep's clothing.

"Sammy, I'm scared."

Then, with just one blink of my eyes, everything snaps back into perfect reality. Sam's face is the same dopey grin and the lights, along with their shadows, have retreated into their normal places. The breath hits my lungs hard and I realize I haven't inhaled for a hot minute. I gasp for air and it stings while my head spins from the quick intake of oxygen. Sam's face drops with sudden apprehension. He pauses, and then his face crumples in distress.

"You fucking weirdo, Holly. I'm just joking. God dammit. Your energy is really negative. It's making me feel negative." He puts his hand over his eyes and lays down next to me. His sleek brown hair fans out on the sheets and you can see the small brown mole on the side of his head where it's shaved. I can't stop staring at that mole right now. It's like it's pulling me in. As my breathing begins to slow I lean in really close and carefully poke the mole.

"….Why?"

"Don't hate me. I love you."

He peeks through his fingers at me. "I love you too, psycho."

I flop down on the bed next to him and let my long, blond wavy hair splay out above like his. "Do you believe in aliens?"

"Why are we talking about aliens?"

"Because, I am one."

Sam re-covers his eyes with his fingers and giggles. "YOU are an alien?"

"Yeah, I mean, I've been thinking about it and I kinda have alienish features and my skin is really thin where you can see all my blue veins and I have all these weird brain problems-"

"So you jump straight to 'alien'?"

"I don't know. Maybe an alien-human hybrid."

"You really are high."

"Just answer my question. Do you believe in aliens, Sam?"

Sam moves his hands away from his face and looks into my eyes directly, his pupils swollen. Actually serious for once, the golds and browns of his irises shine in the light of the TV in the background. "I do. But I don't think they have ever come here. All those UFO sightings…Why would they come here and just fly around? Or just anally probe humans? Makes no sense. I think the universe is full of trillions of other life forms and we are just vain to think they would ever be interested in us or we would be the only ones in this vast universe."

Pressing my knees up to my chest, I close my eyes. "I completely agree. What makes Earth so special and humans so special?"

I hear Sam snicker as I start to drift off, "then how did you get here, oh great Alien Queen?"

2

With an unexpected start, I am wide awake. This is triggered by Sam rolling over and his arm conveniently landing hard on my chest like a dead weight. I groan loudly at the impact but Sam just responds with a pathetic whimper and rolls back over. I rub my chest and grimace, trying to focus my eyes on the room around me. My brain is still booting up like an old eighties computer monitor. The dull orange and gray light from outside trickling through the blinds signaling the beginning of a new day only fills me with a creeping sense of anxiety.

"No… no day…" I mutter as I sit up and pick the crust from the corners of my eyes. My face feels swollen, like I had cried way too much the night before. Knowing me, I probably had. The night before is a muddy mess, fuzzy images, but the feeling from them gone. I look over at Sam's passed out body, drool dripping from his mouth. Without alcohol or drugs, this person feels like a stranger, someone I can't relate to or have any feeling for. I am suddenly incredibly uncomfortable in his presence, in this vulnerable morning moment. With my brain now at least fifty percent functional, I slip on my shoes by the door, grab my purse, and quietly creep out.

The building that Sam lives in was an old hotel from the forties that had been bought and made into cheap apartments. The units may have been lazily redone to look like somewhere you might live, but the hallways had creepily been left almost the same. The stained carpet and wallpaper make you feel like you're walking through a haunted maze that is from a bygone era of phony class.

Since it's early Sunday morning, I am left alone in this hallway. The silence rings in my ears as I try to make my way to the stairs that lead to the main lobby. Everything feels slightly tilted, my fingers brush the walls for balance. I look down trying to make the vertigo disappear. The geometric patterns in the carpet help me to keep one foot in front of the other. I feel like a small child trying not to step on the lava, jumping from crack to crack in the sidewalk. The tip of my shoe finally hits the rubber edge of the first step that would take me down into the lobby. I slowly raise my eyes to the empty foyer. Dusty, plush couches and armchairs crowd the area, accompanied by mismatched side tables. What used to be the front desk stands deserted and feels hauntingly vacant. The whole room gives off a vibe of *there is definitely a little girl's ghost here that wants to play some weird creepy game.* I tiptoe to the front doors that have been jimmied with a haphazard code system in place and, still facing the desolate room, I push the doors open while backing out. *Fuck this place.*

I am immediately greeted with the streets of Long Beach, which are just as unwelcoming. A homeless man is sleeping next to the front door that I don't notice, until he mumbles loudly after the sound of the door shutting behind me disturbs him. I cannot see most of his body due to a dirty tarp, but I can definitely smell that he has peed himself. How? The smell is just that strong.

As fast as my stubby legs can take me in these poorly chosen heels, I rush to my car parked halfway down the block. Luckily, I made it before street sweeping started, so I didn't get ticketed. I kneel on the pavement, cringing slightly at the asphalt on my bare knees, and dig through my insanely large purse for the ever-elusive keys.

"Stupid fucking purse. Stupid fucking keys." I groan to myself. I find my cigarettes first and pull one out of the pack, my hands slightly shaking. It snaps like a flimsy fall leaf. My head drops and I immediately smash it into the car door with my hand. Some of the tobacco sticks to my damp palm and the filter, along with the crushed paper, falls to the ground. A dull pain warms my hand. It feels good. I press my forehead to the door of the car and pause briefly while I grit my teeth in preparation. I push back and then let go, slamming my head into the door. The first hit I feel nothing, just hear the sound. The next hit, I can start to feel the sharp pang followed by the pain. Spreading like sweet relief, every blow to the same spot increases the relief. The warmth. The release. I am hoping no one is leaving for work this early and seeing me in my psychotic display of insanity.

Finally, breathing heavily, I stop. Resting my cheek against the door, I feel my head throbbing. I feel light and, for a moment, I have forgotten who

I am. Then it floods back. This time when I reach in my purse, my hand a little steadier, I take a cigarette out without destroying it. I light it and find my keys. They were right under the fucking pack of smokes. *Oh well.*

I stand up, a little woozy, and get into my old 1994 Thunderbird. I love this stupid car more than I love most people on this earth. You could hit a tree with this thing and barely leave a dent. It's like driving a tank.

I turn the rearview mirror to examine my face. Instant mistake. There are a few splotches on my forehead where the blood is already starting to rise to the surface, and my eyes are rimmed in red skin. It looks like I blew a blood vessel in my right eye.

"At least I don't have a boyfriend that anyone could suspect was beating on me…" I whisper to myself as I jam the key in the ignition. I turn my head around to make sure I don't hit the car behind me as I try to get out of this terrible spot I somehow parallel parked in when out of the corner of my eye I see a dozen small black crawling…things. I whip my head back around, almost forgetting to slam on the brake. *Nothing.* There's nothing there.

3

They say sometimes you can drive somewhere and not even realize how you got there. I guess it's called "White Line Fever" or "Highway Hypnosis." One moment I was driving down Ocean Boulevard after collecting myself into a halfway normal human, and the next thing I know, I am in front of my apartment, several miles away. A cigarette, completely burned out, hangs from the corner of my lips as I grip the steering wheel so hard my knuckles are the shade of white you only see from untouched snow. The stereo is still blaring the same pathetic, warbling song on repeat. I don't know how long I have been sitting here with the engine running, listening to it. I can definitely tell you though that the sun is much higher in the sky than when I left.

I close my eyes and they sting like I haven't blinked in awhile.

When I open them, the world feels distant and cold. Everything is tinged a sad blue color, like I'm looking through a lens. I don't feel human. How am I this living thing with a body? This mind that operates everything, *that* is me. How was it that my consciousness was put in this specific body? My life has existed and has been lived for twenty-five years; I have a personality and thoughts. I feel like the universe is too large and is too overwhelming right now. I can sense the bones in my hands and feel the thoughts forming in my mind. These sensations are not pleasant.

I toss away a dead cigarette and light a new one.

I rub my left hand with my right hand and it doesn't feel normal. The soft flesh on the hard bone is…wrong somehow. I'm becoming anxious; I want to rip my skin off. All of a sudden everything I touch feels soft on the outside but hard underneath. My chest feels like there's a brick in it. My heart pounds.

I am a person. I am a living thing. I have a brain and inside it is me. This is my body.

I shut off the car hastily, crank the window up, and grab my purse. I need to turn off what's happening. I walk quickly to the gate for my apartment building and jam the key in the lock. Swinging the door open hard, it bangs against the wall. I turn around and kick it again just to hear that satisfying *bang*. I then rush to my front door and hurriedly open that one as well. I care not for the "no smoking rule" in the apartment and take my cigarette inside with me. It's my fucking ex-husband's name on the lease anyway.

I mean, he isn't my ex-husband yet, but that's only because he won't sign the damn papers. Every single time I manage to get that human-slug to answer his phone, his pathetic, whiny voice drones on about how he'll sign the papers as soon as he can and how things are just so HARD right now. I couldn't manage to stir up any empathy for that trust-fund baby if someone held a gun to my head.

I drop my gigantic purse full of crumpled trash and fake adulthood by my front door and collapse on the couch. I'm exhausted from just existing. I muster the energy to turn my head towards the television and stare at my distorted reflection on its black surface, this massive shining black reminder of my failed relationship all bought when we moved in together. Nothing is truly mine. I just claimed it like the "bitch" he decided I am. It doesn't matter what indiscretions he may have committed, like sexually assaulting me in my sleep because I am his wife and he should have complete access to me at all times. To him and his family, I was the bitch that kicked him out. I was the one that wouldn't play by these insane, antiquated rules. When his mom wanted to know why we were getting divorced, she put her foot behind my tire so I couldn't leave until I told her why, and in front of his poor nine year old sister too.

I want to stop thinking about this stupid shit so I search frantically for the remote. *Drown it out, drown out my mind please.* I click the pleasing red 'on' button, and that black reminder blinks into a brightly colored swarm of faces. I don't care what show or movie it is, it just has to be anything that will shut off this never-ending thought parade.

I focus all my energy on trying to enjoy whatever soap opera is on right now. Whatever it is, it's awful. I laugh to myself occasionally about just how awful. Finally, as my brain slows and my eyes glaze, I slip into sleep where I am finally far away from the troubles that await me whenever I should return.

4

My phone is vibrating against my forehead. I must have rolled onto it in my sleep. I lift my head up and open my eyes to see a blurry screen with the barely legible 'SAM' lit across the top. I knock my phone onto the ground with a grunt and let my head fall back down. I would prefer getting intoxicated alone tonight. I might have some Norcos still, or maybe half that bottle of whiskey from last weekend. Who cares? Whatever will make me feel like a person for a while. I am hanging precariously on the edge of the couch and roll over onto my back. *Ugh, the ceiling.* Fuck these dumb ceilings that are stucco nightmares. Looks like millions of tiny mountains. I don't understand the point. I have the sudden urge to find a ladder and scrape this stupid ceiling smooth.

It's dusk now. I slept pretty much the entire day away, not that it matters any. I just live off the hush money my ex gives me to keep me quiet. No need to have a job, no need to contribute to this society that spins endlessly around me. I barely fuel my pathetic existence as it continues to be, just to numb my pain all day and night in my LED lit, self-made hell.

With the sun drooping further and further in the sky, the orange light stabs daggers through the blinds, mixing with the glare from the television in my dark living room. The light flickers in between shot after shot of some unintelligible reality show. Their smiles are as fake as their tans. Their laughter has been practiced in front of mirrors. It feels like a rock has dropped onto my chest again. My breathing becomes uneven and shallow. I don't want to look at the walls and most of all, the ceiling.

The shadows are here.

They spread from the corners of this prison of a room, sinuously crawling with every twitch of light. I try not to move. Maybe if I don't move, they can't get me. This reasoning is insane; hallucinations aren't T-Rexes. While neither are real in this apartment, I can't just make up laws for something that my brain is creating out of misfired neurons.

Trying to ignore the sense of impending doom and trying to not look anywhere but the ground, I crawl toward the front door where I know my purse is. Digging through the mess I manage to find my beautiful, little, orange pill bottle. I dry swallow four Klonopin and dig my clenched fists into my eyes. Lights and fractals start to pop because I am pressing my eyeballs so hard; my teeth clench so tightly, they might crack. Everything feels like it's on edge, about to snap.

All I can do is wait for it to pass, wait for the Klonopin to soak into my system and lull my brain into temporary peace. Most people are terrified of the concept that "nothing lasts forever," that all their relationships will end and their beauty will fade, but that phrase is the only comfort I have during a manic episode. While my thoughts barrage me like rapid fire I try to scream internally over them: *NOTHING LASTS FOREVER, THIS WILL END!*

In overwhelming frustration, I begin to cry. This is definitely ugly crying, if not the most hideous version of the thing. Every breath is a gasp for air, which I immediately heave back out as if the burden of inhaling and then exhaling is too much to handle. My face swells as if the tears are coming faster than my eyes will allow and they are backed up behind the dam. Oh, and the snot, never forget the waterfall of snot. Even though my body is doing the disgusting dance of emotions, the release is better than any sex I have ever had. With every sob the world becomes clearer, sharper. The hallucinogenic fog I'm trapped in finally starts to lift.

Thank God for the Klonopin.

By now night has settled around me and the room is completely dark, except for the television which is now playing some game show with a host that just absolutely loves to smile. I wobble to my feet and start the arduous task of turning on every single light in the apartment. I love the safety of my fluorescent bulbs that envelope me in their false warmth and empty comfort. I smile at nothing in particular. It's amazing how much a few lights can change my mood in a matter of seconds.

My face is still crusted in bodily fluids and swollen, but the thunderous storm in my own mind has finally passed. I feel completely exhausted, like I just ran a marathon and every muscle is worn to the bone. Completely drained emotionally and physically, I wander into the kitchen and open my freezer. The blast of frigid air is beyond welcome right now to my raw, hot face. I grab my precious bottle of whiskey and hold it against my swollen eyelids. I don't even bother grabbing a cup or chaser before sprawling out on the couch with my best friend for the night. With the first gulp, I shudder from the taste. I hate the way whiskey tastes, but the aftermath is worth it. Do I care that I am mixing alcohol with my Klonopin? Absolutely not.

I grab the remote and change the channel to a show about women murdering their cheating husbands. *Perfect.* Another gulp and I start to feel a warm burning in my chest. *Warmth.* The thing I can't generate for myself. I will gladly accept these self destructive methods to achieve just fleeting moments of warmth. I start to cry again. I have no idea what I am even crying about.

5

I'm basically paralyzed, completely numb, like every inch of my body is too heavy to lift. Even my eyes seem impossible to move. Their lids are too heavy from another night of tossing and turning.

The nightmares are back. I knew they would be; it's not like they ever truly leave. The memories are foggy, but the residue of depression they leave behind weighs me down indefinitely. Who knows how long this time I won't bathe, how long I won't leave this bed.

Having no control over what I see in my sleep, I shudder at the flashes of memory. His face is always crystal clear in my nightmares; it's as if my brain wants me to suffer. Once I wake up, my mind obsesses over the images and words on repeat like a record skipping. No amount of internal screaming can cover the noise of my own intrusive thoughts. The sound in my own mind is so deafening that I am in near physical pain. I close my fingers around my palm and, with as much strength as I have, slowly dig my nails into the sweaty and vulnerable skin. The actual physical pain runs up my arm and the blaring sound of every thought in my head gets softer. It's temporary relief at its finest. It's cheaper and faster than drugs, even though I'll keep doing those drugs too.

My phone is vibrating: *SAM.* I don't want to move to answer it, I feel too weak. I can't keep ignoring him though; it's been days since I have picked up the phone. With too much effort, I press the little green answer button and the speaker button.

"What?"

"Why are you ignoring me?"

"I'm currently dying. What do you want, Sam?" I am staring at my ceiling, completely zoning out.

"How long have you been in bed?"

I sigh and genuinely ask, "when did I last see you?"

"Five days ago."

"Then it's been five days."

"I'm coming over."

"Please don't," I say in a much darker voice than before. This is starting to annoy me.

"If you have been in bed for FIVE DAYS, that means you haven't eaten much of anything, showered, gotten dressed, or taken care of jack shit. Am I right?"

".… maybe." I roll my eyes to myself.

"I'm coming over and bringing food. If you don't eat, you'll die."

"That's the plan, let's see how long it takes."

"Knock it off." My phone goes quiet, taunting me that the battle to continue my solitude is over. My frustration gives me enough energy to roll onto my back and rub the crust out of my eyes. My chest feels like it's full of bees, very angry bees. I want to just be left alone. I don't want anyone to come and attempt to cheer me up, fill my ears with false words of "you'll feel better if you just get up! Things aren't so bad! Some people have it much worse. Blah. Blah. Blah." As if those words will magically remove all the pain.

I blindly reach over to my side table and feel around for my pack of cigarettes. My throat feels raw from chain smoking all night long, but I put another one between my lips anyway and light it. The room fills with tendrils of gray smoke. It weaves around my fingers up to the ceiling. Everything I own reeks. I reek. It's all cigarette smoke.

My fingers brush against my face and it feels so coarse with grime. I run my thumb over my dry lips; they are so cracked, they are peeling off. I sigh, and out comes more smoke. The decision to try and be presentable for Sam's arrival is a difficult one, because I honestly could give less of a fuck. But more so, I could really do without an hour long lecture about my garbage monster status.

I peel my clothes off my skin. My unwashed body has so many layers of dried sweat on it that when touched it feels like slime. I grab clean underwear from my dresser, or what I assume is clean, because who really knows anymore. It all stinks like cigarettes anyway. The bathroom feels like it's miles away; every step is longer and more difficult than the last. The exhaustion from depression plus the exhaustion from not sleeping has combined and hit me hard. My toes drag on the carpet. I feel weighed down, like I'm wearing twenty layers of soaking wet sweaters. My hand grasps the door frame to the bathroom and I toss my clean underwear under the sink while pulling myself forward. I step onto the cool linoleum that is covered in the same layer of filth that I am, and I glance at myself in the mirror. My throat tightens in immediate regret. I barely recognize myself behind the streaks of filth on my face from all the crying and cigarette ash. My usually glorious hair is ratted up in a nest on top of my head. I am overwhelmed with the deep desire to tear my skin off.

I hurriedly stumble into the shower, desperate to forget what I just saw in that fucking mirror. I instantly feel relief the second the hot water hits my skin. I bury my face in it, silently praying the water would melt my skin away. I let the water run down and drip from my chin, like a glutton. The water is getting too hot; I can feel my skin burning and turning red. I fantasize this is my baptism. When I spit, my saliva is stained brown.

6

Sometimes, I feel like I'm not the one behind the wheel of my own brain. Sometimes, I feel like I don't get a say in the thoughts I think. I'll be minding my own business, getting dressed or driving home, when all of a sudden my brain fills up with the worst thoughts imaginable. They're broken memories that I can't quite remember, but the edges of them still torture me. His face, his fingers, that song…Over the noise of myself, the only way I can make it stop is to scream. It feels like I am screaming an awful lot these days.

I can hear Sam pounding on the door, but I am back in bed and I know that he knows where the spare key is hidden. If he is going to invite himself over, the least he can do is let himself in. Eventually, everything goes quiet for a minute before I hear the door open and Sam's grumbling down the hall. I can feel him behind me, glaring a hole through the back of my skull. I don't want to roll over.

"Holly?"

I don't understand why he had to come over. I was just fine without him here. Why can't he leave me alone?

"Holly, are you awake?"

"Smells good." Sam throws the bag on the bed next to me and leans over so he can see my face. He tries to catch my eyes, but I look straight through the wall as if I can't see him.

"I got you a burger." He nudges the bag closer to my face.

"You really didn't have to do this Sam." I feel too tired to eat a stupid burger.

"Stop being ungrateful and eat it." I finally look at him. Sam needs to blow his nose. I push myself up so I am sitting and immediately I feel a searing pang of resentment. I hate Sam. I absolutely loathe Sam for making me do this. He is a fucking cunt and I wish he would die. I grab the stupid god-damn fucking bag that he is so proud of and tear it open. I pull out the burger inside and immediately my teeth clench so tight I swear my whole jaw cracked. *Tomatoes.* Sam knows I fucking *despise* tomatoes. I look Sam dead in the eyes and I can feel my hatred and anger radiate through my body, giving me an energy I haven't felt in days.

"TOMATOES?!"

"Holly…" Sam holds his hands up like he is surrendering. He knows what's coming.

"YOU KNOW I FUCKING HATE TOMATOES!" I am squeezing the burger so hard it might be turning to liquid.

"I swear I said no tomatoes Holly, I know you hate them." He tries to speak in a low voice, but I can hear the tremor in it.

"I CAN'T BELIEVE YOU! WHY DIDN'T YOU CHECK?" I can't stop. It's like a runaway train, like someone turned the knob to eleven and broke it off. I am a volcano. I don't have the wheel.

"I am sorry, we can just take the tomato off."

"FUCK YOU, NO! THE JUICE IS STILL THERE!"

"I will go get you another one."

"I JUST WANTED THIS ONE TO BE RIGHT!" Without even thinking I smash the burger into the wall. Instantly, as if the smashing magically drained my rage, I snap into hysterical crying: crying, crying, always more crying.

Sam has been by my side through wave after wave of destruction for years. He's like the coast of Japan that has been devastated by tsunamis: rugged but still standing. He sits on my bed crossed legged, eyes wide, eyebrows furrowed, and mouth slightly puckered. He's holding it in like he always does. For me. For my sake. Always for my sake.

"Get on some medication Holly. Some real medication, not just the Klonopin prescription." I am stunned into momentary breathlessness. Sam gets up slowly and walks down the hallway. I hear the front door slam. The only things he leaves behind is the crinkled fast food bag, the smashed burger, and the scent of Old Spice.

I leave my wheel willingly. I float back in my mind further and further until I can't even feel myself.

7

I think my mental illness was confusing for my parents because I was a very happy little kid. Up until things went bad, things were pretty good. I started out as a very sweet baby that could make anyone's ovaries burst. I had big blue eyes and blonde curly hair; my whole family melted when I was born. My dad would record videos of me nonstop as a baby and a toddler. The videos stopped though as I got older. The tapes became lost in the piles of boxes in the garage. My family slowly started looking at me differently, shame and disappointment heavy in their eyes.

I'm not surprised. There were so many times when I was a teenager that I scared my whole family. I did things I'm not proud of and let myself get into all kinds of danger. I would get hurt physically or emotionally and everyone would say "oh well well, if it isn't the consequences of your own actions." As if I didn't know what I was doing. Like I wasn't constantly self destructing and choosing to do so. I was angry and frustrated and felt so alone in this world. Even my best friends didn't get me.

I let a boy get the best of me. I let him ram a knife through my heart and fell apart. I let him be the straw that broke the camel's back. One day I couldn't find him after school, and I knew he left to go to his house and bang this girl he'd met over spring break. I felt used. I felt betrayed. I was angry. But most of all, I felt alone.

I ran home crying. I couldn't get anyone on the phone, not even my mother. So I sat down with the tear stains fresh on my face and took a hundred and fifty Aleve pills without a single emotion. When the ambulance came they told me I "shouldn't do this over a boy." But this had been a long time coming. This wasn't a few weeks of going insane, this was years and years. From the moment a boy turned me into a sexual object for the first time, I was on a one way track to the mental hospital. I had no idea how long or hard I would fall. Turns out, no one would be there to catch me. And it turns out Aleve isn't poisonous.

8

He is using way too much tongue. I wish I had never called him over, but I hadn't talked to Sam in a week and I was feeling despondent in a way that was driving me psycho. It had gotten to the point where I couldn't even feel anything; everything felt far away and fake, like in a dream. Even now, with this guy on top of me, it still doesn't feel real. I put on a very good act though, because I was done and wanted him to finish quickly. All the writhing and moaning I figured would end this sooner than later.

I look at the ceiling. That. Stupid. Stucco. Ceiling. The one that always brings shadows. The ceiling that is all too familiar in any house or apartment. One that I can focus on while some entity plows my hole. I can lose myself in my thoughts and forget that I am, once again, just a body to someone.

He makes a weird sound and stops moving. I sigh. *Finally, this is over.* I push him off and grab my pants and underwear off the floor. As I start to pull them on, this lump of a person that should honestly be thanking me right now for allowing him to do what he did to me, starts huffing and puffing like I had just offended him in the greatest way possible.

"What?"

"You don't want to cuddle?"

"No. Can you actually leave?"

"WHAT? I thought you'd want me to stay the night!" He continues to sit his naked asshole on my couch with his cummy penis almost touching it.

"Okay, seriously, grow up. What would even make you think that?"

"Wow, Holly. You make it really hard for someone to like you."

"I DON'T WANT YOU TO LIKE ME." I pick his shit up and throw it in the direction of his mortified face.

"....fine." He puts his clothes on in silence as I completely dissociate from what has just happened. When the door shuts, I finally breathe and the tears pour down my face before I can even think about what was going on. After what feels like a hundred years, my phone starts buzzing. I look at it hopeful, thinking maybe Sam has finally forgiven me. Nope. Just more bad shit. My ex-husband is calling.

"I can't deal with this right now!" I snort all the snot to the back of my throat and spit it out in the ashtray.

"Why not? What's happening?"

"Honestly, it's none of your business." I laugh, not because it's funny, but because I can't believe his audacity.

"That's not very nice." His voice sounds darker, more agitated.

"I'm not trying to be rude, but I don't need to tell you anything anymore."

"Don't rub it in, Holly."

There's a pregnant pause so thick, I believe I could cut it out of the air. "What do you want?" I continue without really caring..

"My lawyer got all the papers we need, finally. I just need you to stop by and sign them."

I am stunned. "Woooow, are you going to sign them too?" My voice is thick with fake sincerity.

"Of course. That's what you want, right? To be done with me?"

I am officially over this conversation. "Yes. I want this to be done…I don't want to talk anymore, I'll stop by Saturday." I look in my mirror and flick an eyelash carelessly off my cheek.

"Wait, Holly. D-do you need any more money before then?"

I pause. I hate this part. I know it's just him trying to butter me up, keep me happy longer so I won't report him and he won't have to register as a fucking sex offender. "…Yes. Just send me whatever you want. Bye."

"I lo-" I hang up before he can say the worst three words he could possibly utter out of his disgusting mouth. My eyes swell up with tears and I scream several obscenities through my gritted teeth at my now quiet phone. *Love* me? He doesn't *love* me. He NEVER loved me. The last time I saw his face, I was driving away from his parents' house where I dropped him off two mornings after he sexually assaulted me for the final time. The last night he spent in the house, he slept on the fucking floor like the dog he is. Remembering his tear stained face while he begged me to stay together, while also fully admitting to waiting until I was drunk to assault me while I was asleep, it's all too much. It's too much pain for me to have to see his face again to sign these papers.

I'll go though. I've waited so long for him to get it together. I can't possibly postpone it any longer. I won't let him beat me by letting us stay married a second longer than necessary. He's already beat me at this game so many times.

9

The rhythmic tapping of my heels on the pavement makes me feel so powerful. My body never sways with confidence the way it does when I have heels on. My dress might have been too short and too low, but I didn't care. It was Thursday and the money had hit my account. I was ready to drink. I wasn't just ready to drink; I was ready to get fucking PLASTERED.

I live pretty close to my favorite bar, Ferns, so before I could finish a cigarette I was already there. The security guard gave me a wave and I smiled back with a nod. I knew everyone here and they sure as hell knew me. See, Thursday was also karaoke night. I love karaoke and I sing almost all night long, especially the more drunk I get. I want to finish my cigarette before going in, so I lean against the brick building and start looking through my phone to pass the time.

"Holly!"

I look up and see my friend Cody. She's twenty-seven and has a little kid at home, but she never misses Thursday night karaoke for anything. Her hair is long, straight, and brunette; she's wearing heels too.

"Oh my god, I was just about to text you to see if you were going to show tonight. I really want to do B-52s."

"Of course I would come." She giggles, "it's Thursday, bitch"

"Fuck yeah it is." I laugh and drop my butt in the ashtray before following her inside. We head to our normal booth in the back of the bar, and in one second, I go from having a great night to feeling my stomach drop out my ass. There he is, at *our* table, the guy I banged just the other night.

"Cody, I can't go over there." I grab her arm and stop her before she can say hi to this disgusting beast.

"What, why not? It's just Jim. I thought you liked him!" She pulls away and laughs.

"Oh my god, I did like him, until I slept with him and now he is disgusting."

"Wow, that bad, huh?" She furrows her brow and looks at me with concern.

I start to slowly inch behind her and try to pull her to the door. "Yes, that bad. Please, let's go down the street and just forget karaoke, okay? They have pool at Redd's."

Cody turns around and breaks into a smile. "But I want to do karaoke, *please*?" She pouts and turns around to go to the booth anyway.

"Fuck shit asshole bitch." I follow her whispering curse words under my breath.

"Hey Jim."

Jim looks up and sees me standing behind Cody. "Oh hey, I was waiting for you!" I roll my eyes and sit at the spot in the booth the furthest away from him as possible. "I like how your dress looks." Jim says as he openly gawks at my cleavage.

"Why don't you shut up?" I hiss at him.

He looks shocked and then he smiles again. "I'm just complimenting you. I'll buy the first round." Jim gets up and walks over the crowded bar.

"Fuck you, Cody." I hiss quietly at her, squinting in disgust.

"Fuck me? This is SO not a big deal. You fucked him and didn't like it. Get over it, you're not going to ruin Thursday night karaoke because of whatever you did. I want to have a nice night, dammit."

I shake my head. "I don't like him. I get weird creepy vibes from him."

"Then why did you fuck him, dumbass?" She looks at me expectantly, with one eyebrow raised. She wants some great answer that isn't "I'm lonely!" or "I'm stupid!"

"I wanted to." I look down dejectedly, grabbing my own hand and rubbing it for comfort.

This was clearly not the answer she wanted because she huffed and stood up. "I'm going to grab one of the song binders. I'll be right back." I watched her stomp away like I was the one who was just wildly inappropriate. Then a large shadow looms over the booth and I realize why she is in such a bad mood.

"Hi Steven, I didn't know Cody invited you." I move over on the bench so that he can squeeze in.

"She didn't invite me, necessarily. We're kinda fighting right now." He laughs hesitantly.

"Oh, well, shit. Why did you come?"

He looks at me with an innocent smile. "I just wanted to have a nice night, she'll forgive me when she sees me."

Now I smile sweetly because I see Cody coming back; her face drops when she realizes who is sitting next to me.

"Steven, I really don't want you here, what on earth are you fucking doing?" Cody squeezes into our side of the booth and looks around Steven at me. "Did YOU invite him?"

"No, Cody, I just want to have a niiiice niiiight." I look at both of them, batting my eyes. "Now please evacuate this booth, I have to pee and you are squishing me to death." Cody glares at me and gets up with Steven. I push past them as fast as possible and make a beeline for the bathroom.

The women's bathroom at Fern's is entirely pink: pink tile, pink toilet, pink sink. When you're wasted, it's the best place to throw up. Right now, it was just a pink prison I can't escape because the second I leave I'll have to deal with way more things than I am mentally capable of handling. My hands are shaking as I try to breathe. I really wasn't planning on seeing Jim again. I don't know why I didn't think of this. He frequents this bar just like I do. Stupid, so stupid, like the second I'm done with him in my life, I just hope he disappears. But NO, now he's sitting at MY booth with MY friends about to enjoy MY karaoke. I dig my nails into my palm and just try and focus on the pain. Someone knocks on the door.

"One second!" I pull my fingers away from my palm and you can see the raw moon-shaped imprints. I groan and unlock the door; on the other side is Cody, looking very smug. "Oh god, what Cody?"

"Jim brought the drinks over! C'mon!" She grabs my wrist a little too aggressively and drags me back over to my personal hell.

10

I've never been so unbelievably drunk in my life. After Jim bought the first round, he bought me several more rounds of my same cheap, shitty beer. I was never suspicious because I opened all the cans myself, but I should have known he was up to something.

Cody is on the tiny piece of wood they called a "stage," singing some warblish type Fiona Apple song that I'm jiving to. Jim took this as an invitation to dance with me, which it absolutely was not. He keeps pressing his sweaty body up against mine and trying to place his disgusting lips anywhere he can. I keep pushing him away from my face while telling him, "I just want to dance, let's just dance." But that doesn't deter him in the slightest. I can feel his hot breath, his clammy skin; I want to just roll over and die.

Cody's song is over and she's finally gotten out of her trashy mood from earlier. She sees me and concern spreads across her face, but she just frowned and turned away. It was like the beer had soothed everyone into accepting this completely abnormal behavior.

I push Jim away, hard, and quickly run over to our booth, sliding in next to Cody so there was no room for anyone else. "Hey, Cody, we should go home." I look into her eyes trying to convey the horror movie I am currently going through.

"Hey! No way, we should go back to Tony's house!" My attempt has failed; she has no idea how bad it is. Or maybe she does, and just doesn't care enough.

"Cody, I don't want to do cocaine tonight."

"Holl-EE, I WANT to and the night isn't all up to YOU." She looks, sounds, and smells drunk.

"Oh god dammit, you stupid bitch." I suddenly feel warmth behind me and flesh pushing against mine.

"Make room, Holly" Jim guzzles at me with his drunk mouth.

"Fuck OFF, Jim" I turn my head, trying to face my body as much away from him as possible.

"Well, the plan is Tony's and I need coke so, let's go, please." We look into each others eyes, daring the other to blink first and show weakness. I'm way too drunk to play this game. "HA. We are going."

"Me too. I want to go." Jim huffs, getting his breath and spit all over the back of my neck.

"Whatever." Cody nods while looking down at her phone. I want to strangle her. I want to strangle her so damn hard until her eyeballs popped out. I try to make eye contact with her again, but it was too late. The damage has been done. We are going to do coke at Tony's and Jim's coming along.

♦♦♦

Steven is setting up the lines for everyone. I am staring at my feet, wishing I hadn't worn heels, or this dress. I wish I'd worn sweatpants. But we all know it doesn't matter what I wear. Jim hands me another closed beer. I open it and drink it. I don't need this beer, but honestly, with what's happening around me, I NEED this beer. Jim sits next to me and puts his hand on my thigh. I push his hand away, but not forceful enough, because it goes right back where he left it. Except this time, he boldly tries to shove it further up my thigh. At this point, I'm so drunk I can barely see. I try to shove him again and it's barely anything. "No, no, no," I gurgle out. No one looks at me. No one is trying to help or stop anything that is happening. Jim is emboldened by this. He shoves his hand all the way up my dress and tries to force himself into my underwear. "No!" I try to shout, but once again, I'm just so drunk it comes out as nothing. No one looks or notices. Steven does his line of coke as Jim's fingers enter me.

♦♦♦

Steven and Cody decide it would be a good idea to take me home. Jim wants to come. They don't say no. Not only that, they sit him in the back seat with me, with all of me. I sit in fear, wishing more than anything I could disappear; but instead, I'm just absolutely paralyzed. We arrive at my apartment and Jim says, "I'll take her inside"

For the first time all night, someone steps in and Cody says "no, you won't."

11

I've been afraid of the dark for as long as I can remember. It all began when we lived in our rental house just outside of my hometown. I had a bunk bed that I loved to death. The top bunk was a bed and the bottom bunk was a desk, all built for me by my grandpa, who I loved like a father. But when the lights went off at night, I would stare at the ceiling in the darkness and hear voices. Three different voices told me three different things. It frightened me, but I kept it to myself out of fear of something worse: judgment.

Eventually, we moved to our house in Huntington Beach, which was a townhome. This meant that our new house was three stories tall, unfortunately. One bedroom was on the bottom floor next to the damn garage; the other two were up on the top. My brother was younger, so he got the bedroom next to my parents. I, on the other hand, got the nightmare room. The room where if someone broke in, I'd be murdered first. That room terrified me. I always imagined monsters coming from the garage or someone kidnapping me through my window. This led to my door never being closed and my lights always staying on. I couldn't have scary movies, tv, and books because the nightmares got so bad. I was the only kid who never got to read *Goosebumps* or see the newest horror film. I slept like this for years, even into my twenties, living in fear not just while sleeping but during every waking moment. I was always on guard.

I learned as I grew up, there's so much more to be afraid of than what can come out of the dark.

12

Nightmares can feel so real. You wake up and that sick-to-your-stomach feeling is still there, aching, dragging you down. I have slept even worse since separating from my ex-husband. He took away any safety I felt in my bed. I lost any peace had gathered since my parents had kicked me out.

When I wake up multiple times a night, I almost choke on the lump of fear in my throat. The fear that someone is touching me, molesting me, hurting me. No one is there to do those things any more, but my ex-husband made my life hell for months. Even when I asked him to stop touching me in my sleep, he never listened. The day I confronted him is burned in my memory, how he just wept and said that he waited until I was too drunk to wake up. *Too drunk to wake up.*

After being asked to stop, all he did was wait until I wouldn't wake up and fight back. I couldn't believe what he admitted to me. I wanted to smash his creeping fingers, break every single one. Instead, I just dropped him off at his mom and dad's. He'll never face a day in prison, he'll never be on a sex offender list, his future wife will probably never know what he did. But it's burned into MY memory, FOREVER.

I'm awake, AGAIN. I turn over and look at my phone. 3:11AM glares back at me as if it is taunting me. I am so angry I almost throw my damn phone across the room. I don't though, because it's literally one of my only possessions that didn't come from my ex-husband. I treasure the few things that are really, truly mine. Instead, I punch myself on the leg several times in frustration. *Why? Why can't I just sleep? Why can't I just forget? Why on earth am I like this?*

I climb out of bed and, using my phone's light as a flashlight, I dig through my end table to find my small bottle of sleeping pills. *Take one.* Ha. *Take five. Maybe more. Maybe not.* I was still fighting the lump of fear jammed in my throat. *If I can just sleep,* I think to myself, *just lay back down. If I could just sleep.* A small annoying voice in the back of my head starts whispering to me, *You took too much, you might die if you go to sleep.*

I ignore the voice. I push it down and feel myself starting to care less and less about everything, not just about potentially dying. I just don't care anymore.

13

My phone is vibrating. I'm still alive. I search inside myself desperately for any feelings. I'm neither relieved nor upset that I'm still alive. I try to reach for my phone, but before I can even roll over I feel the intense need to vomit. I'm too weak to run to the bathroom so I just grab the trash can under my desk and throw up in it. I feel disgusted with myself as I sit hunched on the floor, spit dripping from my mouth. At least I feel SOMETHING. I throw up several more times before I can even think about my phone again. *Who is calling me this early?* I return to the warmth and safety of my bed and curl up in the fetal position with my phone in my hand. It's Sam. I almost break down in tears. How dare he ignore me and then call me right now, waking me from the dead?

I spend the next several minutes dissociating at the wall, trying to think things through. Should I call Sam back? He is my only friend. I really can't afford to lose him right now. But I feel like this person isn't good for me. Someone that only sticks around because he has no one else besides me. We are two broken people that just trauma bond with each other since no one else would dare get close enough.

Thoughts of Sam suddenly leave me and I'm left with an eerie feeling in my gut. *Oh God. What day is it?* I look at my phone screen and see the worst possible thing I could see on this already dismal morning. *It's Saturday.* My heart starts to beat hard in my throat and I gasp for air that only seems to strain my breathing further. I have been dreading this day all week, and it's finally here.

I pull myself from the warm nest of my covers and place each of my feet on the carpet as slowly as possible. I procrastinate with every movement of my body. I'm a mess already; I can feel this going south. I can feel this being the end of me. *Dramatic bitch.* I sigh to myself, but it comes out as more of a choking bird sound as I catch myself from sobbing.

My phone vibrates again. I catch my breath in my throat. *It's him.* Why is he calling me? I'm on my way, I swear. I'm just having difficulty motivating myself and this phone call isn't helping. It's making me even more scared that this is going to go badly. I cautiously lift my phone, press "answer," and put it on "speaker" before bracing myself for whatever's coming.

"So you're avoiding me?"

"I'm not avoiding you, I just woke up." I look over at my clock and see that it's eleven in the morning. *Shit.*

"I've been calling all morning, I'm coming over to you instead of you coming here. I need to pick up some of my stuff."

"Okay…what stuff? We already agreed on what each of us can have."

"Just like my Playstation and stuff."

"Um, okay, you can have the Playstation, I guess, but what else?'

'We'll talk about it when I get there."

I anxiously pick the skin around my thumb nail. "I'd prefer we didn't. I'd prefer if you'd say it right now."

"I'm hanging up and heading over. Please don't be mean today." I hear the quiet hiss of a phone call become silent. The feeling of bricks in my chest returns again for the thousandth time. I am weighed down by this new turn of events. *What is he up to?*

I grab the clothes off my floor and mindlessly start throwing them in the hamper. I don't want him to see how filthy my life is. He doesn't get to have a win on that one; my life isn't something people get to observe and use to make them feel better about their own shitty lives. I feel like I'm trying my absolute best and something like that would take my self-esteem back decades. I start cleaning off my desk. *I'm doing my best.* I whisper to myself from the quiet corner of my mind where nice thoughts stay. I begin throwing all the trash away, tossing it a little too violently at the trash can under my desk. I feel my anger levels rising; my irritability is completely unchecked. *Why does he get to do this to me?* I seize my sheets off my bed and shake them out, letting crumbs and ash fall to the carpet. I'll vacuum that in a minute, I'm busy getting the visible shit done. Who knows how long it will take him to get here? He could be here any minute and then I'm fucked. I rush through the rest of the apartment, picking things up and throwing things away, when I hear the faint knock on my door that sounds like it's from a coward. Just a slight *tap tap tap,* as if it's from someone afraid.

"One minute!" I yell from the bathroom. I dash to the door and look through the blinds on the window closest to me. I am stunned out of my breath. It's not just him, but his entire family. His entire fucking family and a girl I've never seen before are HERE. She's holding his hand and smiling, like she's having a great fucking time coming over here to bother me. I go for the door knob and pause. *Should I be doing this?* I'm home alone and he has a whole army. But I don't think I have a choice. I feel trapped and small with the door knob in my hand. Finally I turn it to reveal the huge mistake I just made.

14

I sit on the couch, signing the divorce papers and watching my ex's family carry all my beloved belongings out the door. Comforters, the tv, even a bookshelf with my dvds on it, they grab it all greedily. The new girlfriend keeps giggling; I'm about to throttle her out the window.

"I need the computer, Holly." I turn around so my eyes can find the source of the voice. He is standing behind me, lording over me, like he is so much better than me at this moment.

I laugh and say, "what are you talking about, we already discussed the computer and who would get it. We agreed it was me. Remember?"

His mother stops what she's doing and drops the box she's holding a bit too hard. She swings around and stares me down, hatred in her eyes. "If you don't give it to him we are calling the police."

I am startled by her comment and laugh again nervously. "What are you talking about?"

"We. Will. Call. The. Cops. Give it to him now!" She exclaims as she starts walking towards me, hand out.

"Absolutely not, it was even a present!" I get up from the couch and stare her dead in the eyes. "I am NOT giving my computer to you. I want to talk to him alone." I point at my ex-husband, who is still holding his new girlfriend's hand and acting like nothing is wrong.

"We will wait outside, but seriously," she turns to him and smiles a cold, dead smile, "you better get that computer. Or I'm calling the cops."

In hindsight, I should have let them. It's only his and my name on the lease, they weren't even allowed to barge in like they did. But they already did, and I'm scared of what they would do, so I let them in.

"So, let's pack up your computer, I saw the box still in the closet." He starts off towards my bedroom and I grab him before he can leave.

"I'm not giving it to you." I let go of his arm and grimace at him. "You promised me it was mine."

"My mom wont leave without it." He frowns back at me.

"Well, frankly, fuck your mom and fuck you."

"I asked nicely if you could just not be mean today; this is really hard for me."

"Hard for YOU? HARD FOR YOU??" I start pushing him to the door. "Wait outside, I'll pack it up and bring it to you. I just want you out of my apartment."

He looks at me hard and finally smiles. "Fine, I'll let my mom know she doesn't have to call the cops." He grabs the divorce papers off the couch and turns to walk towards the front door. He stops and hesitates before looking back at me. "Please just hurry, I want to get out of here as soon as humanly possible." He opens the front door and leaves, slamming it just a little too much.

I immediately start crying. Fuck him. Fuck his whole family. I'm so done with this situation and the way he gets to manipulate me with his money. I grab my desktop computer and forgo the box. I walk to my sliding glass door leading out onto my balcony and open it with my elbow as I carry the computer.

How dare he feel so entitled to my things, things I worked hard for. So what if he has paid for some of my things? He doesn't own me. I am not a fucking object.

I am not. A. Fucking. Object.

I step out on the balcony and look down at the family all waiting for me. "Hey, assholes! Look over here!" The second their heads all turn I swing the computer over the railing and drop it thirty feet to the ground. The sound of the computer smashing against the pavement makes me sick. It sits for a second before the entire family brings their eyes back towards me. Their faces warp with anger and they start charging towards my door. I run to the front door and quickly lock it so they can't come back inside and torture me or god knows what. The mother starts banging against the door, screaming my name. I drown her out with my screams back: "How dare you come to MY apartment and fuck with me! Get out of here before *I* call the cops on *YOU* for trespassing!"

I hear a brief silence and then some more muffled yelling, but this time directed at my ex-husband. I cautiously step away from the door and back myself into my bedroom. I light a cigarette and flop on my back into the bed. I sigh something like a sigh of relief, but it feels heavy, like my heart is being weighed down. My phone vibrates incessantly against my hip in my pocket. I can feel the anger through the vibrations. I chuckle to myself and turn my phone off. I can't do this anymore. I'm officially over it. I close my eyes and drift off into a restless sleep. Maybe I'll call Sam when I wake up and apologize. Maybe…or maybe I just need some help.

15

I'm emotionally exhausted, but I slept better last night than any night in my whole life. I slept like a baby on Ambien: without a care in the world. I slept like I'd literally passed on from this world and was floating down the river Styx. For the first time in a long time, however, I don't wish I was dead. I feel like I've got a new lease on life; maybe yesterday's events changed who I am at my core. No longer a wimpy pushover, I feel like I'm a warrior. I'm a woman who won't take guff from some pathetic man.

I'm still laying in bed with my eyes closed. If I open my eyes, it'll be over. This happy moment will pass and leave me with my reality, where everything is still fucked. My ex husband is certainly coming after me in some capacity. I now have no computer. Sam still hates me. I hadn't heard from him in weeks.

I groan and roll over on my stomach, smash my face into my pillow and scream as loud as I can. I scream so loud that my throat feels like it's tearing in half. It feels like my throat is on fucking fire, but I keep screaming. When I am finally worn out and feel like I've screamed sufficiently, I roll over and look up at my ceiling. The shadows come out, no matter the time of day. I am so sick of feeling like this. I'm sick of letting this THING take over me.

I'm done. I grab my phone, and I laugh in my head. *What the hell.* I Google search for local therapists. Several names pop up. I start filtering through the options when my phone vibrates. A tsunami of butterflies crushes my stomach.

SAM

Epilogue

I'm standing in front of a tall, daunting, brick building. A building that I will become all too familiar with. I smoke a cigarette and look at my phone. *Five minutes.* I'm so close to answers, to a real life that isn't full of tragedy and heartbreak. I wonder what this new therapist sounds like, acts like. Will she be kind? Will she tell me the things I need to hear to heal? Or will she be so disturbed by my behavior that she'll reject me as a client, rejecting me as a human being. My nerves are high this morning and I puff my cigarette like I just can't get enough. I look down at my phone again. *One minute.* My chest is on fire with anxiety; I have no idea what this woman will say when I tell her everything I've done. She might be so shocked at how I've been behaving she might commit me. Maybe…

I drop my cigarette to the pavement and crush it with the sole of my shoe. I am ready. I'm ready to tell someone what's going on. I need to heal. I deserve this for myself. I deserve to not live everyday choking on my anxiety. I look at my phone for one more second to check the time and smile to myself. It's time for my life to truly begin.

About the Author

Alysa has been writing since 2000 when they started their first serial killer book and tantalized their classmates. This began a couple decades of writing screenplays, stage plays, comics, and books while attending art schools and later dropping out. Instead of continuing with academics, they embraced their love for everything creative—expanding their mind and fulfilling their spirit by creating constantly. These days, Alysa spends most of their time writing, doing freelance social media consulting work, and spending time with their dogs and husband. Don't think that they are living a quiet life though; they thrive on chaos.

They have been mentally ill since '91 when they were spit out into this tortuous world. Writing so their brain doesn't explode. A manic jumbled person with manic jumbled thoughts. Continuously trying to make life a little less lonely, one book at a time.

A lover of dogs, milkshakes, and the PNW. A dedicated karaoke artist. Maker of all things cute and cuddly. A nostalgia whore. Obsessed with the color orange and the '70s. Living proof that aliens exist. A comedian and a national treasure. Enigma of the highest order. Gummy candy is the best candy.